MOTIVATION

MOTIVATION
Self-Motivated
Carla R. Mancari

Celestial Literary Group

Motivation: Self-Motivated

The contents of this book are not meant to take the place of qualified medical professionals or therapists. There is no expressed or implied guarantee as to the effects of the suggestions given or the liability taken.

CONTENTS

Acknowledgment

I appreciate the help of Mary Carpenter. She reviewed and edited the manuscript.

I am thankful for the gift of The Minute Meditation revelation and for all of you who it has helped.

Preface

If you are among those who pay big bucks to listen to motivational speakers, *Motivation: Self-Motivated* is written for you. You may become an aware self-motivated individual with the help of the Minute Meditation Practice and an awareness of your Spiritual Heart Center area. You may realize your full potential.

You may find the word "God" used on these pages. The Minute Meditation practice does not rely on any particular concept of God or religion. The truth of your being is realized beyond words and dogma.

Words can be like locks on a door if you get caught up in them. If any particular term raises offense within you, sit with it lightly. Let the profound power of the Minute Meditation Practice and your Spiritual Heart Center self-motivate from within, beyond words.

1

Energy

Before we can get into motivation and what may self-motivate you, it is necessary for you to understand who you are and what you are made of. Let's begin with a review of energy. Energy is what makes the universe and its manifestations possible. In general, vibrating energy causes many varied manifestations in the world.

The universe and all its manifestations consist of vibrating energy. The frequency states of the vibrating energy of consciousness are continually changing. Energy has been defined as positive or negative. In reality, vibrating energy is originally just being pure vibrating energy. It is the use of it that creates the negative or positive.

There have been in-depth scientific studies involving energy. What you may need to know about energy as it applies to motivation you may become aware of during a silent meditation practice (chapter 8). As you progress with a meditation practice, you may become aware as the energy vibration changes occur within your consciousness. You may be aware of the negative energy effect when you are aggravated or tired. The positive may be experienced as a high energy level when you are joyful, and your motivation is high without becoming tired.

You are continually changing the frequency of your states of consciousness. Silent meditation practice may restore vitality by raising your positive energy level.

2

Awareness
Consciousness

Awareness-consciousness is what you are made of. Although consciousness and its contents vibrate, you cannot be cognizant of awareness. You can be aware of being conscious, but you cannot be conscious of awareness.

Awareness

Awareness is calm, silent, subtle, and changeless. The mind cannot grasp awareness. Attempting to understanding the awareness of your being with the conscious mind is an exercise in futility. The mind cannot grasp that which is beyond it.

You cannot be conscious of awareness. Awareness has no self-reflection and no self-identity. Awareness has no opposites, no separate sense of a personal being.

When watching a movie, you are only conscious of the contents appearing on the screen. The screen is the field of awareness. The content is the appearance. You are conscious of the appearance. This is the way awareness exists. It allows the appearance of an image and its contents that are constantly changing, while it, the screen, remains unchanged.

Look out of a window. What do you see? You may see mountains, trees, houses, or animals. Where are they appearing? All appear in the light of day. The light of day is the one thing you take for granted and never consider. You don't say, "Ah, What a beautiful morning in the light of day." You don't say, "Ah, What a beautiful view of the mountains in the light of day." The light of day is not given any thought. Your attention is on the images, not that which allows the images to appear.

There is no "*I*" in awareness, no self-reflection, no self-identity. In awareness, there are no opposites, no separate false sense of a personal being: all arise with awareness, the changeless.

Consciousness

Three layers of consciousness arise with awareness: spiritual, psychological, and physical. Many *states* of consciousness exist within these three layers of consciousness. With the Minute Meditation practice (chapter 8), you may realize your three layers of consciousness and their many states. You descend (incarnate) into this world through the layers: spiritual, psychological, and physical.

The return way is in reverse: from the extreme outer-most perception to the most inner depth of be-ing. One way perceived out, and one way perceived back, from the One to the many, from the many to the One. The Minute Meditation practice is your inner spiritual journey with awareness of your ability to become self-motivated.

You cannot skip any major layer. All serve a purpose. The mistake that is easily made is for you to get hung up in any one layer with its appearances and its many states. This prevents your motivation progress. However, appearances have their own reality that is relative to that state of consciousness.

Three Layers of Consciousness:

1. *Physical-Body Consciousness Layer*

The conscious physical layer is the grossest layer and the most familiar. Being attached to the personal physical sense of a body keeps you in body consciousness until you progress beyond it. It is beyond the body consciousness that motivation becomes most active.

You should respect and care for your body and meet its needs but not worship it. It is what is within you that is sacred. Therefore, keep your body in top condition, and it will serve you well.

2. *Psychological-Mind Consciousness Layer*

The psychological layer is also easy to become attached to and linger in for a long time. This layer, with its different states of consciousness, may contain the possibility of bliss, visions, fortune-telling, and manipulative mental powers of the physical sense layer. Any of these manifestations may be difficult to move beyond. The mind's imagination will conjure up all the powers and principalities that are entertaining, and often ego-inflating.

Some practices are grounded in scientific or psychological models. However, you don't need to get bogged down with scientific or psychological theories. All of the scientific and psychological knowledge you learn on this plane is relative to this Earth plane.

Intellectual knowledge is helpful in specific related fields. Applying mental effort to a silent meditation practice prolongs your moving beyond these states of consciousness. The silent, Minute Meditation practice is a direct path to the awareness of the Spiritual Heart Center area and the One Consciousness with its many states of consciousness. It is here where the seeds of motivation are planted.

3. *Spiritual Consciousness Layer*

Infinite individual expressions of consciousness exist within the spiritual layer. One is yours. You are an individual expression of the One Consciousness, never separate or apart. Your individual state of consciousness changes as you progress with your meditation practice.

The spiritual layer, the One Consciousness, and its many states may not be as easy to realize as the physical and psychological states. The Minute Meditation practice does not ask you to give up the Spiritual Consciousness layer. You are moving through these states of the One Consciousness as your self-motivation intensifies. You do not have to stay in any of these states longer than necessary.

Because of a false sense of being separate – rather than an individualized expression of the One Consciousness – other individual expressions become challenging to understand. Ignorance of the One Consciousness causes manifested evils and wars on this plane of opposites. Individual conscious mind personalities can change and progress. Consciousness is not set in concrete. Your realizing this would allow your self-motivated interest to make a smooth transition.

Claim your inherent, spiritual right. Become self-motivated from within your One Consciousness. You are beloved of

God and called into being. You are the Word spoken into life from all eternity.

What greater testimony to God's infinite love for you is there? You are you, not someone else. In the entire cosmos, there is no other like you. Being self-motivated means when seeking to realize the One Consciousness, you accept, allow, and respect all manifesting individual expressions of consciousness, as you would respect your own.

3

Mind

The mind is that which is referred to as thinking, memory, feelings, and emotions. In reality, there is no such thing as a mind. What rises in consciousness are thoughts, memories, feelings, and emotions, and they are called "mind."

As vibrating energy rises as thoughts, memory, feelings, emotions, etc. within consciousness, you receive impressions through a physical sense body form (organs) and identify with the impressions. As there is no mind, in reality, there is no person. However, when the thought, "I, Me, My, Mine," rises, you identify with the mind's contents as an individual separate person. This is how the mind acquired its mastership. As a result of a separate false sense of self, you have accepted a master that is a false concept.

As the personal "I" dissolves, you may become aware and distinguish the unchanging in the changing, the inactive in the active. The false fades, as it has no substance in reality, leaving the mind to translate whatever it is your motivational spiritual state of consciousness has brought forth. Concentrated, the mind's rising vibrating energy may be a powerful force. However, your real self-motivational power is beyond the rising vibrating energy of mind.

You may falsely believe that you, of yourself, possess power through the use of a mind, but greater is the motivational power of the One Consciousness. The rising thoughts, memories, feelings, and emotions are rising in consciousness. Consciousness is rising with awareness. Since all rises with consciousness awareness, all motivational power emanates from within you.

As you awaken to the reality of awareness, you will find that the mind and its concentrated power is your dutiful servant. The mind's rising contents are of great use in the service of self-motivation. The world's conditioning, which you feed the mind, affects its response; and its response affects the physical sense body. As a fully awakened being, the heart and mind become one, and the mind's contents serve your true nature.

Conditioning is usually accomplished with labels, names, and identities given to persons, objects, feeling, thoughts, and emotions through repetition. As an aware, conscious being, you have a mind, thoughts, and senses (hearing, taste, touch, sight, and smell) which has a natural power to receive impressions through the body organs. The thoughts and impressions are stamped with the conditioning in the culture or society you live in.

You are conditioned in thought, word, and deed from the moment you enter this world of opposites. Conditioning is continuously being done by parents, friends, peers, authority figures, environment, and culture. Your moral judgment is based on the conditioning of what is considered to be right or wrong according to an established culture or religion.

Because shapes and forms of objects are constructed for use, you are conditioned to think of and see their practical application, rather than to realize their essence. For example, a block of wood cut from a tree, then carved into a chair or table, is always seen and thought of as a chair or table. However, it remains the wood (tree/seed), and if it were burned, it would be ashes. The chair or table is only a functional concept of its reality.

When using conscious sight and thought, you see and think "chair, "table." You are not aware of purely seeing. You see a concept; thus, you do not realize pure awareness. If you are not in a state of awareness, your belief is in the conditioned sense impressions.

Conditioning creates practical, functional labeled concepts (such as a chair or table) for communication and for identifying objects and individual beings. However, it also may create false concepts of thought patterns and sense impressions — all of which you want to bypass when self-motivated. From the time you are born, your conscious mind and physical body are given a name. Repeatedly hearing your mind and body addressed with the given name causes you to identify with it as who you are. You are taught to use I, me, my, and mine, which become personal attachments to the name. All are concepts.

All the impressions made on your consciousness, whether suppressed or repressed, must rise. There is no such thing as an unmanifested consciousness. Therefore, any impression on your consciousness, given space, will rise. Because conscious mind is vibrating energy, you can never dispose of, get rid of, or take away that which has been impressed upon your consciousness through your thoughts, words, or deeds.

Good or bad situations or conditions impressed upon your consciousness will rise whenever given the opportunity. Any thought, word, or deed goes inward not out. Your consciousness' energy vibrates out, but its final destination is always, "Return to Sender." There must come a time when you turn within to allow your consciousness' content, negative or positive, to rise and become purified (chapter 4). Consciousness restored to its original pure state, without opposites, is again freely available for self-motivation.

4

Forgiveness
and
Purification
Restoration

Just how powerful is your Spiritual Heart Center (chapter 6)? It is powerful enough to ignite the forgiveness-purification process. Powerful enough to restore your misused (polluted) energy of thought, word, and deed. Powerful enough to restore within you a pure heart.

Purifying your thoughts, words, and deeds begins with you. You are always working on yourself. Sweep your house (consciousness) clean, and your thoughts, words, and deeds will manifest from a pure heart. A pure heart *is a* self-motivator. It need never seek a motivational trigger outside itself.

Forgiveness-purification is the best possible way to help prepare you for being self-motivated. "As you sow, so shall you reap" (also known, in the East, as "Karma") is an operating law on this earth plane of opposites. It is a reaction to your every action, positive or negative.

All misuse of your energy in thought, word, and deed must be purified through the forgiveness - purification process. The Minute Meditation (chapter 7) may initiate the forgiveness-purification process. It takes you directly to your Spiritual Heart Center.

Forgiveness is secular. It is the gift of your nature that may be given freely and causes no harm. Forgiveness covers you and everyone who may come to mind. The prefix "for" translates away, apart, off. One of the definitions for "give" is to inflict punishment. To forgive is to do away with the punishment or not to inflict punishment.

Forgiveness is not easy to comprehend or to put into action. It has been said, "I will forgive but never forget." You cannot talk about the forgiving part without talking about the "not" forgetting part. It is your choice to forgive or not to forgive. The power lies in forgiving, *and* in the forgetting (the hurt/pain inflicted).

If you believe you have forgiven, but you are not forgetting (the hurt), you are recreating the hurt all over again. To forget does not mean you will no longer remember. Your memory stays intact, but when the memory again rises, the hurt will not rise with it. There will no longer be a negative emotional response.

The emotional suffering and attachment to the event will have dissolved in the wash of forgiveness - purification. True forgiving is forgetting (letting go). The emotional wounds you inflicted or received are healed. The memory of the event is simply that, a memory. It is the discomfort, not the event; you can forget in forgiveness.

Forgiveness touches every phase of your life. It allows the purification process to cleanse and purify your energy, rid yourself of judgment and bitterness, and release negative impressions in your consciousness. If you do not move beyond holding on to old hurts/impressions, you deny yourself the blessing of forgiveness-purification and the direct access to self-motivation.

Forgiveness-Purification

Forgiveness always begins with you. Holding you at fault, being ashamed, accepting blame, and neurotic guilt must come to a space of forgiveness. This space is provided for in the Minute Meditation practice (chapter 8). Then, when the thoughts of your hurts and sufferings rise, and you gently return to your Spiritual Heart Center *area*, forgiveness-purification occurs.

A present hurt (or past one) may have occurred once. With memory, you manage to repeat and repeat, duplicate and duplicate the original hurt many times over. Memory intensifies your pain and suffering. Memory is the reason the same thought (hurt) may rise many times during a Minute Meditation practice. Each time this occurs, it is not the old original hurt but one of the many *you* have created.

The most critical work of forgiveness is not to take back (recreate) that which has been forgiven by responding through dialogue. Absolution *is* absolute. Once you have forgiven yourself, or others, the painfully attached emotions no longer exist.

Prepare to completely give up all that you have held on to and have been attached to, and accept the forgiveness that has occurred during a Minute Meditation practice. Accept forgiveness and allow forgiveness-purification to manifest in your life. Forgiveness-purification gives you the power to release others, and it releases you from your hurts through memory. It frees you to move on; to self-motivation or not.

Forgiveness is like a soft blanket that covers everything and gives you a warm, joyful spirit. It brings a most beautiful calm peace, a pliable peace that penetrates your entire being in all that you are and do. You are the one who ultimately benefits because self-motivation flourishes in a calm, peaceful environment.

5

Your
Spiritual Supply

Your spiritual supply is the DNA of your being. It is the blueprint imprinted upon your soul. Your spiritual supply manifests as insights, revelations, realizations, and material needs. The quality of the fruits that it bears is reflected in the maintenance of your daily meditation practice (chapter 8).

As you gradually realize your spirituality, you gradually realize that the nature of God in spirit and truth may be expressed as your spiritual supply. Your spiritual supply may remind and guide you on your motivational life's journey. It may tend to help keep you on a sound motivating footing. Everything you think, say, and do are indicators of how you translate your motivation into your life. Spiritual supply is the truth revealed through love, kindness, and patience with yourself and others. Eventually, the line between inner and outer worlds is obliterated.

Spiritual Supply

As you progress in living your practical life on this earth plane, your inner world is reflected in the outer. Your spiritual supply responds to the self-motivated attitude of your intentions. The manifestation of your spiritual supply may cause confusion to occur when you are sure of what should manifest in your life, but it does not.

When you have done all that is asked of you, and all of the signs indicate that what you believe your desire *will* manifest, should manifest, but does *not*, a deep abiding confusion may set in. It is a confusion that may throw your life into devastation, despair, and distrust. It may cause distrust in your self-motivation skills.

When the desire you want is at your fingertips, and yet you cannot grasp it, it seems to be the trickery of the highest order, one that you do not deserve. You are tempted to seek others to motivate you. There is a tendency to forget that it is *your* consciousness that manifests whatever *you* need. Others may assist, but it is *your* consciousness that must ultimately manifest what is necessary. Yes, your consciousness may overrule your hopes, dreams, and the best of intentions.

Your consciousness is your best guardian angel, protector. Your consciousness may interfere with an obvious manifestation if it is not in your best interest. Always it is your welfare that is being protected from any manifestation that would retard or interfere with your life's progress.

Although it may be your intention to fulfill a desire, your consciousness is aware that a fulfilled desire may be more devastating to your life than one that is not. Not getting a desire that has all of the appearances of manifestation may easily cause a mental state of confusion and distrust. The mind may find it difficult to cope. A fulfilled, motivating desire is only a temporary fix. Another desire is quick to rise. Fulfilled desires motivate the birth of endless desires to hold you in a disturbing peace and a place of negative bondage.

Negative surroundings bring into view the negative situations and individuals' energy vibrations that you may be immersing yourself in. When situations and individuals vibrate negative vibrating energy, it creates an environment that surrounds you with coarser/slower vibrations. Your motivation weakens.

It is all about choice. You have an obvious choice. It is up to you to become self-motivated, and choose your environment wisely from a pure heart, and your spiritual supply may be activated in your daily life.

Self-motivation is born out of the awareness that there is a spiritual supply that meets your needs—need, not greed. With the awareness of your "spiritual reality source," is your spiritual supply. All that is necessary to meet your needs already exists; that includes your motivational intentions. Your supply is a spiritual source that always exists in unmanifested abundance. It is limitless in its unmanifested source state. It can never be depleted.

Money, food, objects, positions, or persons are not your spiritual supply source. These are a few of the forms that the spiritual supply may manifest. Like self-motivation, the peace, joy, comfort, and material supply that you need and seek exist within you. You may realize your spiritual supply with the Minute Meditation practice (chapter 8). As your practice progresses, conscious awareness of the manifestations of your need becomes more obvious. Look around. This earth produces all you shall ever need. There is *no* limit of supply. It is the human manipulation of the spiritual supply manifestation that causes limitations.

The mind is powerful, but it may also be mischievous and can cause havoc on the plane of opposites. To mentally focus your thoughts to fulfill your needs is incompatible with your harmonious spiritual nature. Your supply may appear as persons, objects, and events. Because this is the plane of opposites, you may attract and be attracted to both the positive and the negative forms that consciousness manifests; some you will want, and some you will not.

Resting with the awareness of your Spiritual Heart Center area (chapter 6) allows the things of this world to be appreciated and accepted as gifts to be enjoyed. Your response to them can then be heartfelt gratitude rather than insatiable greed. Choose wisely. There is abundance within you that provides for all your needs. You are a beautiful spiritual being, and abundance is constantly gracing you. The awareness of the natural abundance of all that surrounds you in the world may serve as a reminder of the presence of your spiritual supply. The abundance expressed in this world is but a foggy perception of the greater abundance it reflects within you. You need to be aware, pay attention, and notice the wonders of this world created for your use, and you would be self-motivated beyond expectations

6

Your
Spiritual Heart
Center

There is an old tale that goes something like this: After God had created humankind, God called an angel and asked the angel to hide the one thing God wished to conceal.

"I have finished except for one thing: the mystery of life. Where shall you hide it?" God asked the angel.

"I will hide it in outer space," responded the excited angel.

"No," God said, *"someone will easily find it there one day."*

"All right, I will hide it on the moon. Surely it will not be found there?"

"No, no," said God, *"one day, an individual will be able to look there also. Hmmm, I have it! Let's put it within them. They would never think to look there!"*

~~

There is a gentle, subtle vibrating center within you (in the center of the chest, between the breasts). It's called the Spiritual Heart Center because of the proximity of the physical heart. This energetic, vibrating center is also called your "other heart." The Spiritual Heart Center is known in the East as the Fourth Chakra, Anahata Chakra.

Although often written about and discussed, the Spiritual Heart Center's direct availability and easy access are *often* ignored. It is the most neglected entrance into the inner sanctuary of your being. The Spiritual Heart Center is where the One Consciousness offers the feast of greater awareness of your reality. As you are aware of the Spiritual Heart Center area, you may come to realize the awareness of the One Consciousness where self-motivation may be realized.

The Spiritual Heart Center is the access door to your self-motivation. There is no greater self-motivator than your Spiritual Heart Center. Truth is manifested in your Spiritual Heart Center through the One Consciousness and translated with a purified mind. All mystical mysteries are resolved here, and knowledge, understanding, and wisdom are realized. It is here you may realize your uniqueness — your self-motivation reality. The Minute Meditation practice (chapter 8) may guide you directly to your Spiritual Heart Center, the One Consciousness, and your motivating presence. With a realized awareness of the expanded Spiritual Heart Center, your form may be filled with a consciousness awareness where self-motivation may be intensified.

Swami Rama, one of the greatest masters of the Himalayas and founder of the Himalayan Institute in Honesdale, Pennsylvania, was aware of the Spiritual Heart Center's power. He wrote of an Eastern Spiritual Heart Center contemplation that is passed on orally in secret from guru to disciple. This innermost sanctuary is the "Holy of Holies" of your being.

There are seven spiritual centers (chakras) within the physical body. They begin at the base of the spine and end at the top of the head. These vibrating energy centers are located three below and above the Spiritual Heart Center. The Spiritual Heart Center is the powerhouse that influences the centers above and below it.

This pure vibrating energy center does not have a particular religious affiliation. Members from any religion, or none, may access it. The Spiritual Heart Center connects all states and levels of consciousness.

Fortunately, the Minute Meditation Practice gently guides you to the point where you may access your Spiritual Heart Center. This is your birthright and may be reflected in your daily living. The Spiritual Heart Center's pure vibrating energy is continuously teaching, guiding, and self-motivating you in this world. Practice the Minute Meditation and be aware of your inner sanctuary, where you may realize that you need not go anywhere, nor seek others, nor pay big bucks for motivation, which is always within you.

All the strength and action you could ever desire in your life exist in every vibration of your Spiritual Heart Center. The vibrating energy is an invulnerable power. The Spiritual Heart Center may guide your footsteps to an awareness of your inherent spirituality. Here you may become aware of your uniqueness as a self-motivating individual expression of consciousness.

You may become aware of this power as you practice the Minute Meditation (chapter 8). This power radiates a light that you may step into and with which you may be as One as you rest with the silent awareness of your Spiritual Heart Center. Your spiritual power is a center of compassion, clarity, discernment, and wisdom. The best ingredient for a self-motivated individual is you.

You may become aware that the power to wash away greed and bathe you in self-motivation resides in your Spiritual Heart Center. The power is without limits, and it cannot be diminished. It is a protective strength, an eternal grace that accompanies you on your life's journey and envelops your conscious mind.

You may have been led to believe that the conscious mind is the power to be harnessed. Yes, the mind is a powerful instrument, and when it is focused on the things of this world, it may perform seemingly magical feats and fulfill desires. But the mind, in and of itself, has no power. All it can do is what is given to it from within.

The mind may manifest desired attractions, but it may also cause mischief and create obstacles where there are none. To work only with the mind is to deny yourself the opportunity to go beyond the mind to where the motivational power exists: your Spiritual Heart Center. The power is given directly to you from within. You decide whether to invest the power in the manifestations of attractions in this world. You may use or misuse your power of vibrating energy.

Your full self-motivational potential is not met in a world of noise and chaos. Your full potential is met with the silence of awareness of your Spiritual Heart Center and is manifested in your practical life. It is essential that you turn within to tune into the silence, away from the noise and chatter of this world, for at least one minute twice a day (chapter 8).

The Spiritual Heart Center is the access door to your self-motivation. No code, secret password, referral, or formal introduction is needed to access your Spiritual Heart Center. Within your Spiritual Heart Center, truth is manifested through the One Consciousness and translated with a purified mind (chapter 4). All mystical mysteries are resolved here, and knowledge, understanding, wisdom, and motivation are realized.

With the Minute Meditation, you may realize the power within and hear the silence. You may become aware that with this silence, your Spiritual Heart Center is readily available to you. Here you will bask in the pure, vibrating consciousness with awareness. From here, whatever is necessary to meet your needs manifests without relying on the mind's creations.

The pure vibrating energy of your Spiritual Heart Center can lift you from the most mundane human being to the most motivating, magnificent, natural one. Natural because you are comfortable in your physical being and secure with the world as you reside in it. This energy cradle nourishes and comforts you, affecting all you do and thus allowing you to realize your full self-motivational potential.

It will never be enough for you to know about your Spiritual Heart Center. You will always long to connect to and access it. The Minute Meditation is the boat that will carry you across the river into your Spiritual Heart Center. Get in and take the ride of your life, which will take you to a new beginning of you.

7

The
Minute Meditation

Is there a meditation that can help you to become self-motivated? Is there a meditation that may help you to give up seeking motivation outside of yourself? Is there a meditation without all the time and energy consumption required by most meditations? Yes, there is. It is the Minute Meditation.

There exists a spiritual center (it is not an object or feeling you can experience) at the center of the chest between the breasts. It is called the Spiritual Heart Center and your other heart. The Spiritual Heart Center is where the One Consciousness offers the feast of greater awareness of your reality. As you become aware of the Spiritual Heart Center area, you may realize the awareness of the One Consciousness, where a purer, finer vibrating energy may be realized.

The Minute Meditation practice (chapter 8) may guide you directly to your Spiritual Heart Center, the One Consciousness, and your reality. With a real-ized awareness of the expanded Spiritual Heart Center area, consciousness may be filled with awareness where self-motivation shines. Become a more aware self-motivational individual.

The Minute Meditation (also known as M&M because it is sooo sweet to you) is a revealed life-changing meditation of awareness that may allow you to become self-motivated to realize your full poten-tial. It is a minute of infinite power. It is a minute of profound rest. It is a subtle, calming minute that allows you to move effortlessly to the silent awareness of your Spiritual Heart Center area. It is the gift that keeps on giving.

The Minute Meditation drops the more traditional aids—such as a word, thought, image, sound, or breath—and articulates simplicity. The Minute Medita-tion also drops the traditionally extended periods, rigid posture, and strict rules of other practice regimens. The Minute

Meditation intends to establish you firnly in your spirituality. Your life is built upon hallowed ground and is rooted in love. The Minute Meditation connects you to the awareness of this hallowed ground to realize your inner guidance and achieve full self-motivational potential.

The Minute Meditation allows your inherent "image and likeness" to be restored to its full stature. It supports, strengthens, and deepens your connection with your Spiritual Heart Center. Without extraneous dialogue, stringent guidelines, or complicated definitions, the Minute Meditation bypasses the potential distractions in which the mind loves to indulge.

The Minute Meditation is a practice of "undoing." You are being guided to undo many years of conditioning with the least amount of effort. It is the opposite of what you have been taught in modern culture.

You have been conditioned to accomplish whatever you want; you must "do"—sometimes overdo—to achieve your goal. You push, shove, and drive yourself to the brink to get what you believe you want. Getting and grasping, effort, effort, all is an effort.

The Minute Meditation teaches you to do the opposite. Relax. There is no pushing, no shoving, and no driving yourself anywhere. You simply rest with the silence of awareness of your Spiritual Heart Center area for one minute twice daily. Force and exertion are not necessary. You may receive what you need when you release and let go of the driving pressure.

The most significant effort you can expend is showing up and be patient for one minute twice a day. In the silent awareness of your Spiritual Heart Center area, a minute is an eternity. The mind takes you on an outer journey through the alluring attractions of this world. The Minute Meditation takes you on a direct inner journey through the aware reality of your spiritual nature. When faithfully practiced, the Minute Meditation slowly, carefully, and lovingly connects your inner spirituality to your outer physical life.

A lack of understanding of your spirituality creates distortions. You may be working with conventional mind-body consciousness and the perception of a false sense of a separate self. The Minute Meditation allows you to venture beyond the usual mindset into a sense of your reality with awareness. The Minute Meditation establishes you in the unconditional, nonjudgmental truth that dwells naturally in your Spiritual Heart Center.

Your nature has many facets. Within your Spiritual Heart Center, your inner power's brilliance continuously reveals your spirituality. When you let go and are willing to embrace yet another previously unknown facet of your nature, the life-changing transition is motivational.

The Minute Meditation is a practice for you who are interested in responding wordlessly in solitude, simplicity, and silence for one minute twice daily. The Minute Meditation may connect you with infinite power and profound self-motivation as a path to realizing your self-motivational indwelling nature. All silent meditations may have their value. What is it specifically that makes the Minute Meditation self-motivating?

This silent practice eliminates the middleman—the breath, word, sound, or thought. It's a short, direct path that guides you, without interference or obstacles, to the awareness of your Spiritual Heart Center area. Nothing need stand between you and your reality. The Minute Meditation cuts to the chase in leading you to realize your full self-motivational potential.

The Minute Meditation may require some adjustment of your ideas concerning what "ought" to happen. But the deep silence this practice generates will more than reward your attitude adjustment. Yes, less *is* more. When you begin the Minute Meditation, you respond to the invitation to come home. You are accepting inner guidance.

You are a living presence within a devotional heart. The Minute Meditation carefully and painstakingly takes you to your all-inclusive inner presence. It is a silent, restful journey. The Minute Meditation brings you to the awareness that the mind's attempt to capture, codify, or commercialize eternal life will be brought down. The mind cannot withstand the wear and tear of time, frustrations, anxiety, and disappointments. You become aware that your balance and strength result from inner peace, not external items or events.

The Minute Meditation's inward pilgrimage of the unknown may take you to the knowledge of inner self-motivation.

There is a presence within your Spiritual Heart Center that the world cannot comprehend. Seek it. Go for it!

8

The
Practice

How often must you listen to motivational speakers to motivate you? Why look to others to lift your spirit and move you to realize your full potential? Your Spiritual Heart Center (chapter 6) *is* the greatest motivational speaker. The Minute Meditation of awareness practice may ground you in perpetual *self*-motivation.

The Minute Meditation is an easy awareness practice that you can quickly learn. Sit comfortably on a couch or chair; sitting on the floor is optional. You may lie down if your health does not permit you to practice in a sitting position.

The Minute Meditation may be practiced at any time before a meal, at least two hours after a meal (the changing energy vibration will interfere with digestion), or about an hour after drinking juice. Water is fine. Over time, you will find that your inner practice moves in the direction of a minimum amount of effort. *A word of CAUTION:* Never practice any form of contemplation, quiet time, meditation, or awareness, even for a moment, while driving, operating machinery, or at any time when your safety may be at risk.

MINUTE MEDITATION PRACTICE

1. Sit comfortably, rest your hands on your lap or by your sides, and close your eyes. Slowly deeply inhale; then very slowly exhale, relaxing your entire body. Then continue to breathe normally.

2. Consciously become aware of your Spiritual Heart Center *area* (center of your chest, between the breasts) and rest with the silence of awareness.

3. When thoughts or sensations arise, do not dialogue, converse, engage, or respond to their rising. Your attention is already there. Allow them to be, then return again to your Spiritual Heart Center *area* and rest with the silence of awareness.

That's it. Is that easy enough? This simple, silent, one-minute, twice-a-day practice may help you quickly reap all your inherent benefits to realizing your self-motivation potential.

At the end of a practice period, take a moment to become consciously aware of your mental and physical senses again before returning to your normal activities.

~~

Listen to what an individual who has taken the Minute Meditation challenge has to say about it:

Grahame, a retired postman in Australia, reports on his Minute Meditation practice.

Spending just one minute twice daily from my busy routine does wonders for me. Whenever I feel overwhelmed by the stress of modern living, I take one minute to put it right.

I sit quietly, take a deep breath, and bring awareness to the center of my chest, my Spiritual Heart Center. I allow my awareness to be on this area, just resting but staying alert.

Just one minute twice a day with this practice may alleviate tension. I feel rejuvenated with a new perspective.

The Minute Meditation practice allows me to function back in the crazy world with a new wholeness and vitality. It has brought peace and assurance in my life that I thought not possible. I'm grateful.[1]

~~

Recurring comments from practitioners of the Minute Meditation:

- I sleep better.

- I'm less prone to harbor resentment.

- My children tell me I'm easier to get along with.

- I'm more flexible when things don't go my way.

- I experience more joy in my life and more self-acceptance.

- I'm happier, and my friends say, "You're nicer to be around."

---

1 Letter of permission 2011.

- My emotional responses to life's ups and downs are more appropriate and less exaggerated.

~~

In coming home to themselves at the deepest level, Minute Meditation practitioners report an ability to remember what their lives are all about. By effortlessly resting with the silent awareness of their Spiritual Heart Center area for just one minute twice a day, many say they return to their daily activities with renewed energy and a renewed sense of purpose. Aren't these comments what motivation is all about? Aren't these the necessary ingredients that go into a self-motivated individual? The comment most often made is, "It changed my life." Such reports are an incentive to take up the life-changing Minute Meditation practice and reap its benefits.

Each time that thoughts, emotions, or any of the senses, sight, hearing, smell, taste, touch, seek your attention, gently again become aware of your Spiritual Heart Center area. Repeating the practice, again and again, is not starting over, beginning again, or going backward. It *is* continuing.

Do not label or dialogue internally with thoughts, emotions, or senses that may arise during practice. All thoughts, sensations, and images will fall away if you do not engage with them. For an instant, you may rest with silent awareness.

Internal dialogue is a conditioned response to the conditioned thoughts and sense impressions the mind creates. This is the 'busy work" of the mind. It may interfere with and stall your practice. It is a habit that distracts your attention from being self-motivated. Dialoguing attaches you to past hurtful memories, increases your suffering, and intensifies emotional pain.

Internal dialogue mainly deals with memories and future expectations. It may successfully hold you in the past or trap you in the future—neither of which exists in the present. During practice, dialoguing may cause the present moment of silence to slip away.

Dialoguing is powerfully attractive and difficult to resist. When a memory arises that has anger and resentment attached to it, dialoguing encourages you to step into an emotional cesspool to indulge in imaginary vindictiveness. This causes your vibrating energy to be awash in impurities - negativity.

Internal dialogue serves no useful purpose. It may be given up without any repercussions. N*ot* dialoguing offers the significant benefits of lessening emotional turmoil and creating space for self-motivation progress.

Be consistent with your practice: one minute, twice a day. Do it. To say "I'll try" builds in failure. To *do* assures the possibility of success. Success may come by doing. Trying gives you a way out. Doing gives you a way in—into all that you seek to realize; your self-motivation potential.

If, for any reason, you find it challenging to become aware of your Spiritual Heart Center *area,* place your hand upon your Spiritual Heart Center area (center of your chest, between the breasts) for the first few practice periods. You are not seeking to feel anything. The mind feels. You are resting with the silence of awareness beyond mind-body consciousness.

Be aware that thoughts, emotions, and sense impressions *will rise* in mind during your practice. This is what the mind does: it thinks. That is its purpose. You are not practicing to stop or still the mind. You are choosing not to *dialogue* with the thoughts— to not chase after them—thus creating the opportunity for self-motivation.

Once purified, a memory or sense impression will never plague you again. The energy you would have expended on the memory or sense impression is now available to consciously decide how to use. Be kind and loving with yourself as you practice the Minute Meditation. You will have thoughts; practice is not about having no thoughts. It is about learning to be aware when dialoguing with those thoughts and gently returning to the silent awareness of your spiritual Heart Center *area*.

Do not concern yourself with doing it "right." If you are sitting for one minute twice a day when thoughts or emotions arise, you lovingly return again and again to the silent awareness of your spiritual Heart Center *area*, then you are doing what is necessary. Be flexible. Flexibility gives you the freedom to adjust to new routines. An active, self-motivated individual requires flexibility: any change to a routine can create resistance. All too often, you may be attached to a particular schedule, time, or place. You may want everything to be the same day after day. In most situations, this might seem ideal.

Developing flexibility in your practice can lead to developing flexibility in all aspects of your life. Flexibility is a nurturing skill that will help you to be kinder to yourself. Go with what you have, wherever you are.

You may want to sit for your first Minute Meditation practice in the morning and the second during the afternoon or evening. If you find that fitting in a daily second practice is difficult—you can't find the time because of work, errands, children, and a million other things on your agenda that interfere—this is understandable. Here's a suggestion: you do go to the bathroom sometime during your busy day, right? Stay on the John for an extra minute. It's that easy. Your friend, John, can be very helpful. In fact, John may become your *best* friend!

There is a silence within you that is so deafening that it can be heard. You are silently talking with your other heart when in silence, you rest with awareness of your Spiritual Heart Center area. You may hear a silent voice that speaks to you and motivates you. You may come to hear this silent voice more easily than any voice in this world. The silence is a timeless graced gift of your nature. It is the greatest self-motivator that exists.

9

Practical
Living

Practical living is day-to-day responsibilities, activities, and services performed. A silent Minute Meditation practice is not stopped when you open your eyes and go about your outer activities. In your silent practice, there is the element of mindfulness. You are mindful of all that rises. This mindfulness should be carried into your world of outer practical living. That is what mindful self-motivation may do for you.

Meditation should be practical in your everyday life. The thinking should not be, "this is spiritual; this is not." Judging what is spiritual and what is not is a slippery slope.

Be consciously aware of all you do in thought, word, and deed. Stay alert and pay attention to your thoughts, spoken words, and deeds as they rise, inviting participation on the plane of opposites. If you are aware of what you say before you say it, you may prevent suffering for yourself and others. Acts or deeds will be more appropriate if you weigh whether they are necessary.

What you learn during a silent meditation practice may be practical in your daily living. The no responding, no-dialoguing, and being gentle with yourself may help when you are actively self-motivated in your involvement with others. Do not separate your inner meditation practice from your outer self-motivated practical living.

When you are consciously aware of what you are doing, all activities are spiritual. Washing dishes and scrubbing floors are spiritual activities when you do them with conscious awareness. The One Consciousness motivates and guides you in and out of a Minute Meditation practice. The guidance is seamless.

10

Pondering

Pondering is the art of creating a space between contemplation and meditation. In this world of technology and electronics, pondering is fast becoming a lost art. As an individual expression of consciousness, pondering allows your consciousness to express itself in a safe, quiet environment. It is an asset for self-motivation.

Pondering requires that you slip into a mode of stress-free relaxation. For a time, you give up any intentional thinking and allow your mind to drift restfully. Pondering may move you to ever more profound levels of consciousness. It may help a particular subject of interest as you allow whatever wishes to rise and delve into its motivating possibilities.

You are not engaging or responding to whatever presents itself. You are allowing your own consciousness to present what you are attracted to in the present. It is as though you are watching a gigantic motion-picture screen. Once

80

thoughts rise, they expand or become distinct according to the attention or lack of attention; they attract at any moment.

Pondering contains no sudden mental moves or holding on. It is close to daydreaming, except that you are aware of your pondering content/s. Pondering is something you do when you are alone, restful, and not in a hurry to be anywhere.

The Art of Pondering:

1. Slowly sighing, relax.

2. Keep eyes open but unfocused, allow thoughts to arise, and roam at will.

3. No matter what rises, allow thoughts to multiply or dissipate gently.

4. Take control, if you wish, and explore a particular motivating thought.

5. End pondering whenever you wish.

Pondering does not have to be a planned session. You may indulge in it whenever you find yourself in the quiet necessary surroundings. Pondering gives you a free time out, a time out from the electronic assaults. You may find yourself being self-motivated on a firm footing.

11

Accept, Allow, and Respect

When you get upset and insist that you know better, it's your ego gone amiss. All that you do for others, you are doing for yourself. An act of compassion is a reflection of the awareness of *your* self-motivation nature. There is never any time that you are doing anyone a favor. The favor is for you.

Like a washing machine that agitates dirty clothes, until they come clean, your inner guidance agitates until your vibrating energy is clean. Accept, allow, and respect the choices and decisions of others. The Minute Meditation Meditation is about working with *your* emotions, *responses, doubts, temptations, and* motivation so that you are well prepared to succeed.

Your outer actions reflect your inner individual moral sense of your consciousness. Therefore, to maintain a healthy balance in your outer world, there must be a healthy balance within your consciousness and vibrating energy. That's the work of The Minute Meditation practice (chapter 8).

Your vibrating energy field affects how you are motivated and how you treat yourself, others, and everything around you. The Minute Meditation's direct path of awareness helps you to understand the power within your Spiritual Heart Center, which helps you to create a healthy balance. Your outer life conforms to the inner, not the other way around. You have an inner power that pierces the illusion of an inner-outer separation. It's not separation. It's reflection.

Part of motivating your life is to accept, allow, and respect others' rights to make choices and decisions for themselves so that you can get on with the work that *motivates you.* There are benefits when you can accept, allow, and respect yourself and individuals. These benefits allow you to move beyond any conflicts of interest.

ACCEPT

- Acceptance of others frees you from judging.

- Accepting any given moment reveals the present.

- When you accept others, you accept yourself, which is an expression of self-love.

ALLOW

- You will lose fewer friends if you are patient with those who disagree.

- Choosing not to criticize those with different views will deepen your awareness.

- Allowing others to be where they are reduces expectations, stress, and struggles.

RESPECT

- Respect for yourself and others is an expression of your inherent spiritual nature that may bring about compromise.

- When you respect the beliefs of others, you suffer less from emotional turmoil.

- Giving others the same respect you believe you deserve contributes to a positive state of mind.

~~

When you are agitated by others' behavior, stop, look to yourself, and ask, "Why does this upset me? What is going on with me?" A conflict of interest is at its greatest intensity when you insist on holding on to the familiar while the new overshadows it. A conflict of interest dissolves when you let go of the familiar to welcome a self-motivated life.

12

Mini-Exercises
Helpers

The mini-exercises are offered as helpers as you progress on your inner spiritual journey. Use them wisely.

1. NO-POWER EXERCISE

The No-Power Exercise may allow you to address a particularly thorny recurring issue. However, it is its own unique exercise and is to be used *only* when necessary. Its sole purpose is to remove invested power in an internal sense-impression (a specific tormenting issue of thought, word, or deed that has made a tormenting impression in your consciousness).

The No-Power Exercise does not replace your twice-daily silent Minute Meditation practice. And the exercise is never to be mixed during a Minute Meditation practice. The internal sense-impression may be experienced as a solid steel form — non-penetrable. It may be the most difficult vibrating energy to purify. Because you have given it power by previously accepting a false belief in it, it may be a constant struggle just attempting to make the slightest dent.

The power is directly given to you from within, and you are the one who invests or withholds the power. An internal sense-impression of itself cannot attach. You attach, detach, give it life and death, and you may shed the false image of the impression. You learn to forgive yourself and those who may have done you harm. The No-Power Exercise may bring you into a neutral zone of non-responding and restore your inner peace, an integral part of the exercise.

You *never* use the No-Power Exercise while driving or operating any mechanical equipment. In addition, you do not use the No-Power Exercise whenever your safety is at issue. No exercise or meditation of any kind should be practiced during these times.

This is not a "no" dialogue practice like The Minute Meditation Practice is. When you pronounce *"No-Power God is,"* you are doing a specifically targeted dialogue exercise. The significant difference between a *"no"* dialogue practice (The Minute Meditation) and a specific, targeted dialogue exercise (No-Power Exercise) is its use in the result of taking back your invested power from a particular impression that would not respond during the ordinary scheme of things.

When using it, it is most important to remember the immediacy of responding, *"NO-POWER, GOD IS."* The "NO-POWER" is your realization that the tormenting thought of itself has no power. The "GOD IS" acknowledges that only God is, and God alone exists right there in the moment of the tormenting thoughts rising.

The Exercise:

A. You may internally use the No-Power Exercise as you go about your daily activities. You internally repeat the words, *"No-Power, God Is,"* during your daily outer activities (when there is *no* safety issue) as often as needed and refocus your attention immediately on the external activity. The exercise may eventually restore the vibrating energy to its original state, causing the necessary healing and allowing continued progress on your spiritual journey.

~~

2. HAND-TO-HEART EXERCISE

The Hand-to-Heart Exercise is a quick short-term solution to be used in a time of spiritual energy crisis or needed guidance. Conscious awareness transforms. As you practice the silent Minute Meditation, many inner changes may occur. An expansive consciousness may create times of highs and lows. At times your energy vibrates at such a rapid speed you may feel as if you are on a roller coaster.

The silent Hand-to-Heart Exercise may be used in a spiritual energy crisis or time of needed guidance. Whenever you have a silent practice, purification may bring change, and an inner struggle may occur when there is resistance to change. There may be a variety of inner experiences that are inexplicable at the time. The conscious mind may be struggling to understand the changes that are taking place beyond comprehension.

If immediate help is unavailable, the silent Hand-to-Heart Exercise may be a short-term solution. This exercise may be used anywhere and during any activity. The silent Hand-to-Heart Exercise may help bring immediate calm and may restore your vibrating energy's balance.

The Exercise:

A. When inner vibrating energy turmoil besieges you, rest your hand on the area of the Spiritual Heart Center (center of the chest between the breasts).

B. Take a long deep breath, exhale slowly, relaxing mind and body. Rest your attention on your hand (not on the awareness of your heart center) with the silence of awareness. If necessary, repeat several times.

Do not be fooled by the simplicity of this exercise. Hands are many times used to heal or to bless. The Hand-to-Heart Exercise may be empowered with the essence of your spirituality.

~~

3. The Listening-In Exercise

The Listening-In Exercise is the inner ability to hear the voice of the inner silence. In the silent stillness within your

Spiritual Heart Center, you may come to listen to your rising thoughts. As you rest in your Spiritual Heart Center area with awareness, the ability to turn a "listening-in" ear to hear your inner guidance may increase. The inner silence may become so deafening that it is loud and clear. From this listening-in posture, you may realize that the heart and mind are one.

Over time with the use of listening-in to the inner silence within your Spiritual Heart Center, you may find a silent, sacred language that speaks to you. Discernment thrives in a listening-in environment that allows your vibrating energy to become calm, balanced, and steady. The more you rest in a listening-in mode within your Spiritual Heart Center, the more you may hear. Your inner guidance is always communicating with you. Listen-in, and you may hear.

The Exercise:

1. Whenever you have a situation, condition, or question, you may sit quietly with your eyes open or closed.

2. Place your awareness on your Spiritual Heart Center area. Then, softly, listen-in to the silence. Listen as though you were waiting for a phone to ring.

~~

As you use listening-in, the inner silence deepens. You may find more clarity of perception in the discernment of conflicting points of view. Discernment arises with compassion and quickly resolves a present moment's need. As you progress on your spiritual journey, your understanding, insights, revelations, and realizations may be deepened. When you are prepared and ready to receive, there is not nothing that you are denied.

Summary

Self-motivation is an inspirational interest from within that moves you into action. Self-motivation allows you to study your intent. Hopefully, you have understood what you are made of (chapter 2) and that self-motivation is baked into those ingredients. When you can accept, allow and respect all human beings, your self-motivation will spring forth or rise from a pure heart.

Motivation bought from outside of yourself may fall as quickly as it has risen because you are purchasing it from another's consciousness. Self-motivation springs from your consciousness. You have the necessary tools (chapters 6 – 8) to accomplish this. Practice the Minute Meditation, and you may find that your consciousness is the only motivation coach you need, a coach that is always readily available on demand.

Author

Carla R. Mancari is a prolific author, life guide, and teacher. She leads retreats to improve individuals' (from all walks of life) self-confidence and self-esteem; and enable them to meet life's challenges. For more than 45 years, Carla has guided individuals in understanding life's spiritual principles, spiritual activities, and rising emotions in their private and daily lives. Her greatest joy is helping individuals to realize their self-worth, unique gifts/talents, and full potential *and* to wake up to their spirituality.

Carla is the recipient of The Christ Centered Prayer revelation, The Minute Meditation, and The Heart-Centered Meditation. She is a co-founder of the Contemplative Invitation Teaching. Although Carla had never attended high school and was labeled a retarded child, she attained two University degrees: a B.A. from the University of South Carolina in Columbia, South Carolina, and an MEd from South Carolina State University in Orangeburg, South Carolina. Carla studied at Brigham Young University and attended the School of the Americas in Switzerland.

Carla led a class-action suit in the United States Supreme Court to protect minorities' rights (Morton vs. Mancari, 1973) and was a certified psychologist. She served in the United States Air Force. Traveling worldwide for many years, Carla studied with Christian, Hindu, and Buddhist masters. She was a guest on the Larry King Show and a guest lecturer at various colleges, professional groups, and book signings.

Carla gained national recognition when featured in *Good Housekeeping*, "The Education of Carla Mancari, 1969." It chronicled her life in 1967-68 when she was the first white student to receive a Master's degree from the then all-Black South Carolina State College in Orangeburg, South Carolina.

Website:

www.ChristCenteredPrayerPractice.com

Author's Books

Mancari, Carla R., *When Jesus Is the Guru: A Wayward Christian's Spiritual Walk*. Celestial Literary Group, 2010.

- - - *Eco-You: A Power of One, Improve Your Health, Improve Your Life.* Celestial Literary Group, 2019.

- - - *Walking on the Grass: A White Woman In A Black World.* Celestial Literary Group, 2016.

- - - *The 4th Chakra: Your Spiritual Heart Center – How to Quickly Access It.* Celestial Literary Group, 2016.

- - - *Abortion and The Bible: The Abortion Dilemma: A Scriptural Response, A Woman's Spirituality.* Celestial Literary Group, 2017.

- - - *Racism: The Pain of Invisibility.* Celestial Literary Group, 2017.

- - - *The Rising Emotions: Understanding and Mastering Them.* Celestial Literary Group, 2017.

- - - *The Mystical Path: The Serious Student.* Celestial Literary Group, 2017.

- - - *Spiritual Principles: Understanding, Realizing, and Living Them.* Celestial Literary Group, 2018.

- - - *Climate Change: Consciousness Change.* Celestial Literary Group, 2017.

- - - *Words: Locks On The Door or Keys To The Kingdom.* Celestial Literary Group, 2018.

- - - *Aging: Physical to the Mystical.* Celestial Literary Group, 2018.

- - - *Divine Love: Your Nature.* Celestial Literary Group, 2018.

- - - *The Lazarus Rising: The Kundalini – A Rising Dormant Energy.* Celestial Literary Group, 2018.

- - - *Depression: Hopelessness.* Celestial Literary Group, 2018.

- - - *Jesus Christ: Teacher.* Celestial Literary Group, 2018.

- - - *The Transformation: Change of Heart.* Celestial Literary Group, 2018.

- - - *The Mystical Surrender: Giving In.* Celestial Literary Group, 2018.

- - - *Death Ain't Dead: Empty Graves.* Celestial Literary Group, 2018.

- - - *Common Decency: Your DNA.* Celestial Literary Group, 2018.

- - - *Christians?: Common Decency.* Celestial Literary Group, 2018.

- - - *Beyond Buddhism: Meditations.* Celestial Literary Group, 2018.

- - - *Exit: Get Ready, Set, Go.* Celestial Literary Group, 2018.

- - - *Meditation: Good For You.* Celestial Literary Group, 2018.

- - - *How To Love "You:" Begins with You.* Celestial Literary Group, 2018.

- - - *Consciousness: Yours.* Celestial Literary Group, 2018.

- - - *Suicide: Understanding It.* Celestial Literary Group, 2018.

- - - *Detachment: Realizations.* Celestial Literary Group, 2018.

- - - *Detachment: Christian.* Celestial Literary Group, 2018.

- - - *Sexual Abuse: By The Church – Its Root, Coerced Celibacy.* Celestial Literary Group, 2018.

- - - *Guns and Guts: The Courage To Act.* Celestial Literary Group, 2018.

- - - *Jesus, The Way: A Mystical Understanding.* Celestial Literary Group, 2019.

- - - *Motivation: Self-Motivated.* Celestial Literary Group, 2019.

- - - *Totally Free: Is Killing Me.* Celestial Literary, Group, 2018.

- - - *A 30-Second Meditation For Teenagers.* Celestial Literary Group, 2018.

- - - *A 30-Second Meditation For Seniors.* Celestial Literary Group, 2017.

- - - *The Five Faces Of Love. Celestial Literary Group, 2019.*

- - - *Angel In The House.* Celestial Literary Group, 2019 (A Children's book).

- - - *Put It In The Bible: Prayerful Requests,* Celestial Literary Group, 2019.

- - - *Loneliness: Heartache,* Celestial Literary Group, 2019.

- - - *Hate: A Dark Emotion,* Celestial Literary Group, 2019.

- - - *Greed: It's Addictive.* Celestial Literary Group, 2019.

- - - *On Being Young: Choices.* Celestial Literary Group, 2019.

\- - - *Gratitude: Expressed, Sincere.* Celestial Literary Group, 2019.

\- - - *Humor: A Necessity.* Celestial Literary Group, 2019.

\- - - *A Christian: Are You One?* Celestial Literary Group, 2019.

\- - - *A Habit: How To Switch Meditation Practices.* Celestial Literary Group, 2019.

\- - - *Impeachment: Living On The Dark Side.* Celestial Literary Group, 2019.

\- - - *The Jesus I Know.* Celestial Literary Group, 2019.

\- - - *Grace: Spirit And Truth.* Celestial Literary Group, 2019.

\- - - *Temptation.* Celestial Literary Group, 2019.

\- - - *The Christian Journey: Teacher Student Relationship.* Celestial Literary Group, 2019.

- - - *The Beloved: Who Is The Beloved?* Celestial Literary Group, 2019.

- - - *What Now, Lord? Enlightenment.* Celestial Literary Group, 2019.

- - - *What If I Were Gay?* Celestial Literary Group, 2019.

- - - *Mother Mary: Mother of Jesus.* Celestial Literary Group, 2019.

- - - *I Remember America.* Celestial Literary Group, 2019.

- - - *The Overcoming: "Jesus."* Celestial Literary Group, 2019.

- - - *When Faith Is Not Enough.* Celestial Literary Group, 2019.

- - - *The Plane of Opposites: The Work.* Celestial Literary Group, 2020.

- - - *Crisis.* Celestial Literary Group, 2020.

- - - *Grief: Gut-Wrenching Emotion.* Celestial Literary Group, 2020.

- - - *God.* Celestial Literary Group, 2020.

- - - *Regrets: Do You Have Any?* Celestial Literary Group, 2020.

- - - *1968, 1968,1968: The Mind of A Racist.* Celestial Literary Group, 2020.

- - - *Satan.* Celestial Literary Group, 2020.

- - - *Practice Practice: Meditation.* Celestial Literary Group, 2021.

- - - *Metaphysical Questions With Answers From The Spiritual Heart Center.* Celestial Literary Group, 2021.

- - - *Christians Without Jesus: Prodigal Son's Journey.* Celestial Literary Group, 2021.

- - - *From Here To There.* Celestial Literary Group, 2021.

- - - *An Awakening Path: Christian Spiritual Principles.* Celestial Literary Group, 2021.

- - - *Holy Scripture: Uplifting, Inspiring and Comforting.* Celestial Literary Group, 2021.

- - - *Male Female: The Split Soul.* Celestial Literary Group, 2021.

- - - *The Inner Message: Theological Mystical State.* Celestial Literary Group, 2021.

- - - *A Guide To Understanding Mind's Contents And Realizations.* Celestial Literary Group, 2021.

- - - *A Sister's Laughter: Oh! How I Miss It!* Celestial Literary Group, 2021.

- - - *Churches: Are They Necessary?* Celestial Literary Group, 2021.

- - - *Metaphysical Stories and Poems.* Celestial Literary Group, 2021.

- - - *Jesus, Jesus, Jesus.* Celestial Literary Group, 2021.

- - - *The Disciple and The Mystical Guide.* Celestial Literary Group, 2021.

- - - *The Holy Trinity: 1+1+1=1, No Mystery.* Celestial Literary Group, 2021.

- - - *Fear of Jesus.* Celestial Literary Group, 2021.

- - - *Symbols and Rituals: Christian.* Celestial Literary Group, 2021.

- - - *Christian Minute Meditation.* Celestial Literary Group, 2021.

- - - *Christian Minute Meditation: Pocket Size.* Celestial Literary Group, 2021.

- - - *The Spiritual Heart Center: Pocket Size.* Celestial Literary Group, 2021.

- - - *The Spiritual Heart Center.* Celestial Literary Group, 2021.

- - - *Sin.* Celestial Literary Group, 2021.

- - - *Compassion.* Celestial Literary Group, 2021.

- - - *Silence.* Celestial Literary Group, 2021.

- - - *The Christ Centered Prayer Meditation Teaching Guide.* Celestial Literary Group, 2022.

- - - *Spiritual Zone.* Celestial Literary Group, 2022.

- - - *Bible Scriptures: Mystical Understanding.* Celestial Literary Group, 2022.

- - - *Lead Us Not.* Celestial Literary Group, 2022.

- - - *Let's Talk About Jesus, Or Not.* Celestial Literary Group, 2022.

- - - *For The Love of Jesus.* Celestial Literary Group, 2022.

- - - *Abortion, When Life Does Not Begin! Exodus 21:22-25.* Celestial Literary Group, 2022.

- - - *Morton vs. Mancari: A Plaintiff's Response: How An Average Joe (woman) Landed In The US Supreme Court.* Celestial Literary Group, 2022.

- - - *Christian Spiritual Exercises: The Inner Journey.* Celestial Literary Group, 2023.

Casey-Martus, Sandra, and Mancari, Carla R. *The Lessons, Volume One*: *How to Understand Spiritual Principles, Spiritual Activities, and Rising Emotions, 2nd Edition.* Celestial Literary Group, 2020.

- - - *The Lessons Volume Two*: *How to Understand Spiritual Principles, Spiritual Activities, and Rising Emotions, 2nd Edition.* Celestial Literary Group, 2020.

- - - *The Christ Centered Prayer: Revelation, Strait Gate and Narrow Way, Second Edition.* Celestial Literary Group, 2018

- - - *Your Other Heart: The Best Kept Secret, Second Edition.* Celestial Literary Group, 2011.

- - - *The Scripture Prayer: Praying The Scriptures.* Celestial Literary Group, 2020.

- - - *The Christ Centered Prayer Meditation Practice: Pocket Size.* Celestial Literary Group, 2021.

Carpenter, Mary B., and Mancari, Carla R. *The Minute Meditation, Book 1: It Is Profound!* Celestial Literary Group, 2022.

- - -*The Minute Meditation, Book 2: Workbook, (The Minute Meditation, It Is Profound!).* The Celestial Literary Group, 2022.

- - - *The Minute Meditation, It Is Profound! Book 3: The Essentials.* Celestial Literary Group, 2022.

- - - *The Minute Meditation, It Is Profound! Book 4: A Diet For The Soul.* Celestial Literary Group, 2022.

- - - *The Minute Meditation, It Is Profound! Book 5: The Three of You, You Are*

Never Alone. Celestial Literary Group, 2022.

- - - *The Minute Meditation, It Is Profound! Book 6: Pocket Size.* Celestial Literary Group, 2022.

- - - *The Minute Meditation, It Is Profound! Book 7 – Teaching Guide.* Celestial Literary Group, 2022.

- - - *A Scriptural Reference: For The Lessons: How to Understand Spiritual Principles, Spiritual Activities, and Rising Emotions, Volumes One and Two, 2nd Edition.* Celestial Literary Group, 2020.

- - - *Spirituality: Yours.* Celestial Literary Group, 2021.

- - - *Dreams: States of Consciousness.* Celestial Literary Group, 2021.

NOTES